THE COLOURS OF HEROINES

Nora Patrich

THE COLOURS OF HEROINES

Lydia Kwa

women's
PRESS

CANADIAN CATALOGUING IN PUBLICATION DATA
Kwa, Lydia, 1959–
        The colours of heroines

(Not a luxury poetry series)
Poems.
ISBN 0-88961-199-8

I. Title. II. Series.

PS8571.W32C6 1994   C811′.54   C94-931684-9
PR9199.3.K83C6 1994
copyright © 1994 Lydia Kwa

Editor: Angela Hryniuk
Copy Editor: Nancy Chong
Cover Design: Dawn Lee
Cover Illustration: "Galloping Through Life" by Nora Patrich
Inside illustrations: "Memories" (p. 2), "Anchi Mallen (Virgin Warrior)"
(p. 8), "Awakening"(p. 40), and "Coya and Land" (p. 88)
by Nora Patrich.

Quotes from *Analysis of Chinese Characters* by G.D. Wilder and
J.H. Ingram, 1974.
Definition of *translate* taken from *Chambers Twentieth Century
Dictionary*, 1981.
Quote in "A Taste of Blood," taken from *Interview with the Vampire*, by
Anne Rice, Knopf, 1976. © Anne Rice.
Quote from "There's a kind of hush" by Les Reed and Geoff Stevens,
1966, © Donna Music, Ltd./Leo Feish Inc.

This book was produced by the collective effort of Women's Press.
Women's Press gratefully acknowledges the financial support of the
Canada Council and the Ontario Arts Council.

Printed and bound in Canada
1 2 3 4 5   1998 1997 1996 1995 1994

For Suemay

CONTENTS

Nora Patrich

FATHER:MOTHER:TONGUE

Pasar Malam

On Wednesday evenings they all appear, light from kerosene lamps gleaming off their wares set on rectangular wooden tables. I am walking from stall to stall, seven, ten, then thirteen, in a red dress, white polka dots, black bow across the waist, bust-darts hint at emerging breasts. My awkward green plastic slippers, I pause to shake out stones and sand. We are three, mummy, *bapa*, and me, drifting like loosely formed apices of a triangle, silent, watching. Two lines of temptation on either side. Weekly ritual, trance-like attention to detail, did she have these porcelain dolls, or the fake jade vases, last time? Or that pink nightgown hanging on the third tier?

Food sellers. Heaps of corn steaming in an aluminium cauldron set in a large bicycle-cart. Tapioca flour-cakes, hot and freshly fragrant from the scent of *pandan* leaves placed beneath them, and inside, the dark sweetness of coconut and *gula malacca*.

The fortune teller sits low on a wooden stool, she waits for the open palm, a question to be traced out on a red grid of possibilities. I want to know, will I be rich, will I marry, what kind of life will I have?

Pasar Malam. This night, my window.

Pasar Malam — Night Market
bapa — father
pandan — fragrant leaves used in cooking curries and desserts
gula malacca — thick brown palm-sugar

Hidden Claws

the cats, disdainful monarchs
nestled in the grooved seats
of those mahogany throne-chairs
with marbled backs

it was another time:
grandfather's house where they prowled
geometric three-coloured floor tiles
faded with friction of feet.

I was bigger but the cats ruled
with their hidden claws and
eyes fluorescing in the dark.

uncle roamed the house
with stiff brushes and acrylic paints,
strokes of gold and silver
on antique tables, chairs, sandalwood trunk.
once he stole the key to the china cabinet
glossed the Ming-blue saucers
with green rims and yellow centres
to mimic unripe papayas.

I ran from them all
up the stairs, into my room.

it's been ten years.
my grandparents' ghosts must still be
pacing those floors.
mother doesn't talk about it

but *bapa* says uncle has taken
to the streets, diving
into ill-fated ventures.
clawing hands
that used to pounce at coins
spilling from grandma's money belt,
now curl around other addictions.

I'd like to believe
no cats remain in that house;
when I meet them on the street
I pause to let their flanks move
against me
but I avoid their eyes.

bapa — father

As She Caught Death

*I remember now, I was six. Two weeks before the
festival, my parents, uncle and grandma burned
garbage at the front of the garden after church. They
threw her into the fire, my favourite doll with the one
good blue eye. Blonde curling out from under the red
bonnet flung into the bonfire, her straw insides
crackled as she caught death.*

> lunar festival
> at the Buddhist temple:
> sacrificial pig
> swathed in incense smoke
> waxy pink mouth
> clamped over a tangerine.
> the streets near the temple
> crowded with worshippers
> and curious nonbelievers
> like me, alone at the junction of
> Koon Seng and Tembeling.
> the medium in her royal robes
> silver jungle of hair
> travels past the altar.
> I watch her spin lunar phases
> scatter the crowd
> flick her horsehair wand
> across my face.
> I'm afraid.
> she's bold, colourful
> presence her weapon
> perhaps she has magic
> can bring my doll
> back to life.

Do I remember correctly, that I was alone, since my parents wouldn't have let that happen? What about them burning the doll? No, that's not imagined, but I'm not sure anymore about the sequence of events. Fragments of memory. But the brevity, like a gasp of air quickly held, the body slow to let go.

They call you Luna or Mana, whose worship Christians condemned as madness. O, Moon Mother, silver woman, as she caught death, over the ages, come rescue. Won't you reach into the fire and return her whole to me?

Their Stories

The pot of porridge and ten bowls standing up against the war. My father at twelve is the cook, a Chiang Kai-shek badge hidden in his pants pocket. After interrogation from Japanese soldiers who enter their *kampong* home in Muar, my father and two brothers plan to steal mangoes from the neighbour's garden. On the new moon, they paint their faces black with charcoal, sneak out to rob the trees, load as many fruits as possible into their singlets, fumbling gleefully home. Their mother in Singapore is busy with her new husband and work as principal of a Chinese school.

What do you do with time, as three brothers surviving the war?

Uncle punishes them the next day, a spanner across the face, a dunk under water in the bathroom urn, until they bleed spluttering choking for mercy.

Remember my stories, we had a hard life, eat the crusts of your bread.

My mother's father is a Singaporean businessman during the Occupation. He has special ration coupons because he welcomes the enemy home for banquets served at the mahogany table, in Ming porcelain and English silver. My mother often accompanies the servants to the store where coupons are traded for the month's supply of rice. She understands commerce early on because her father pays her for killing the mosquitoes in his room. His favourite, eldest child of the first wife, suddenly turns serious and reserved after her sister dies of pneumonia.

Remember Kong-Kong? He was rich, had wives and concubines.

They meet in Zion Presbyterian Church at 49, Koon Seng Road. In Katong Park he sings love songs to her, like *Be My Love* and *O Danny Boy*. It doesn't matter that he's poor, that she has fallen in love with someone of a lower class, chosen him over the wealthy match *Mah-Mah* made for her. She tells herself he's a good-hearted man, he'll take care of her. She regrets later the price of love: *Mah-Mah* keeps *Kong-Kong*'s money from her, squanders it on her brother instead.

I want to hear your story again please, about how romantic you were.

He and she. In the 1950s, young and hopeful. Believing that love would be enough. After the war, the memory of survival still glistening on their tongues, he with the receding sting of a slap across his face, she with a life growing in her womb.

kampong — Malay: village
Kong-Kong — grandfather
Mah-Mah — grandmother

First Lessons

in secondary three
Mr. Lam our biology teacher
puny man with hairy nostrils
greased wave of hair perched
rooster's comb
said: *the heart is*
the size of a fist
then placed his hand to his chest
as if in a war salute.

I was taught
biology is destiny
we are forever children
of our parents
and girls must bleed
into women.

you have a heart of stone
bapa said
because I didn't speak
for months to him
except *hello*
when he returned from work
in the evenings.

the doctor asked
to let myself feel
so I confessed *he beats me*

his fist
rammed the backbone
until my heart gave in
first turning soft
then gradually
hardening.

bapa — father

Underneath It All

My earliest underwear dates further back than toilet-training. Those were the days of cloth diapers, and mother organized my collection with militant devotion: every soiled diaper immediately sanitized in a large aluminium basin, steam and soapsuds concealing the process. This is conjecture, based on later memories of her raging battle with dirt.

My own obsession with underwear started with Tarzan movies, the ones with Johnny Weissmuller and Maureen O'Sullivan. What immodesty! Running around in loincloths, swinging from tree to tree. Those movies more exciting than life as a frumpy teenager bundled up in a school uniform. Add a constant tropical humidity, and you too would find fantasizing about loincloths appealing. I never possessed any skimpy outfits. The closest I came was when I played Mother Cat in costume for a school production. I chastized three young ones for having lost their mittens. Far from risqué.

I've heard many women say that when a girl becomes a woman it's an event to be celebrated. It wasn't for me. When I saw the stains on my underwear, I thought I was in big trouble. As usual my mother was squatting over the washboard in the bathroom, when I flashed her my soiled underwear. I didn't understand her lack of surprise, as if she'd been expecting it at that very moment. She led me into the bedroom, initiated me in a hushed, secretive tone, extracting sanitary pads from the bottom drawer as if fragile explosives. I was told I needed to protect myself with those white wads. Against what? How did Jane manage in the jungle without them? What did she use instead? These were details that movie scripts left out.

Uniform

at Tanjong Katong Girls' School
we wore forest-green pinafores
with darts cutting up
toward nipples.

during Free Period
some girls changed
out of uniform
into brightly-coloured shorts
to visit the boys at T.K. Technical.
the same girls who read *Playboy* or
Penthouse at the back of the class
when an article on childbirth was featured.
those of us labouring
with trigonometry at ink-stained desks
heard loud gasps and
snickering, the words of disbelief
that vaginas could stretch so wide
yield blood and babies
at the same time.

the first time I'd heard
the word *vagina*
was at Haig Girls' Primary:
a schoolmate had an accident
climbing over the iron fence
her foot missing a hold
so that a rusty prong
pierced her *there*.

we were warned about fences
some solemnly-whispered words
about being girls still
having pinafores on
a concern that we might not
make it safely.

I didn't understand why
men's magazines would highlight
a woman's pain.
what would compel
my classmates to laugh
impatience throbbing
past their uniforms?

Sinseh Ma

seventy-two and still
she walked long distances on those knobs
of choked flesh, crushed bone
always wore a beige *cheong sam*
white knee-highs
black cloth shoes

Sinseh Ma, our "barefoot doctor"
belonged to no one else
knew secrets of the earth's yield
fruits she mixed into powders and ointments

prayed as she healed
alto inflections of her chanting
radiant moon-shaped face
hair pulled harshly into a bun

hands large, the knowing fingers
insistent waves of heat
travelling to dull the pain
a distance away

her kindest words were for us children
always a gift for the suffering one

even then I wondered, was she lonely?
had she ever given
her body's secrets to someone?

her feet bound in a village in China
at four, blood and bone sacrificed
in the name of beauty
a man's pleasure

even though her feet had prepared her
she never married

Sinseh Ma — Grandma Physician
cheong sam — close-fitting dress with slits up the sides

Travelling Time

I.

now the scientists are saying
time travel doesn't have to be
fiction anymore

space
like dough
worked through by a woman's fingers
ball stretched to a length, until the middle
gapes with air:

hole in time, through which we might
enter another's history
nothing will be the same again

II.

a woman dreams
      of a woman
      in a dark cell
      who looks out of the hole for
      light: the moon
      she could pace, has reason to
      instead she sits still
      she could cry, pray
      but the priest has already come

      she refuses to confess
      in exchange for salvation

      people want to see her
      get what she deserves
      tomorrow she will burn

      tonight she dreams of better times
      memories no one can steal

a woman dreams

III.

it's 6 p.m. Saturday
here where I am
6 a.m. Sunday
half a world away

my parents are probably still sleeping
I'm eating dinner, about to write
a poem

if I were a medium
I could reduce
three thousand miles
cross it like a street

suppose I had that power

a fantasy
given
the Greenwich meridian

IV.

I wake up screaming
no memory of the nightmare

a week later
my father is dead, heart attack
a cold shell found by her at 7 a.m.
when I cut my finger thirteen hours
behind them, hurrying to cook dinner
to make up for lost time

I travel through zones
to sleep in the bed where he died
dream of marshland, menacing and alive
rushing up to drown me

my chest seized by pain
I wake up screaming

Scooter

my father waltzed with cars
weaving in between them
on a *lambretta*
his body and scooter
one sleek creature
slinking through narrow gaps.
he'd bought his first
soon after he finished working
the cargo ships to Indonesia.
cream-coloured with blue sides
and black leather seats
a vehicle for romancing my mother.
after marriage it became
a conversation piece
among their rich friends
a novelty to see us
arrive in shifts: daughter
then wife in the passenger seat.
for church and special occasions
we'd hail a taxi, the three of us
intently watching the meter.
my father couldn't pass the driver's test
and my mother never tried.
it was easy then to trust
the certainty of limitations,
dream of other possibilities
without believing in change.

even now, years after *bapa*'s death
I remember riding behind,

oil and sweat, the odd pungence
of pomade, his salt-and-pepper hair
poking out from under the helmet,
while the colours of people
and streets whizzed by so fast.
as if my father were a magician
as if he could keep waltzing forever
between the gaps.

bapa — father

Who Is She Beyond?

for over a decade oceans
have separated us

I'm trying to imagine her
as a young woman.
I have a photograph
my father took
the year before they married:
at twenty-three, buoyant on the Raleigh
travelling down a dirt road
her long black hair
a frizzy permanent
riding behind her wide smile.

days after my birth
another kind of image
eyes indifferent to the camera
while her arms limply cradled me.
was her hand gentle then
did she kiss my cheek
with regret?

I remember her need
for dirtlessness.
her sense of duty
to dailiness of laundry
flapping furiously on
bamboo poles fourteen floors
above sea level.

while she hung up clothes
she'd tell me stories:
her younger sister died
at four of pneumonia,
her brother kept hauling
my grandmother off
to the psychiatric ward whenever
she resisted
his attempts to steal
from her pockets.

my mother begs me to
forgive and forget,
read the Bible every day.
her pleading has intensified
since my father's death
God will kill me if you don't do this
she screams out, in one of our long-
distance calls.
she is now a litany
of physical pains,
an ancient language
drowning in her cells.

while I am here
flinging questions
into my own constructed silence.
the proof of a photograph
and yet

who is she beyond
obligation?
why did she abandon
her bicycle
and slide so anxiously
into life?

Hardhats And Safety Boots Must Be Worn On This Project

This is the black-and-white taken the day after I left her womb. Her opaque eyes, moonstones directed at the camera eye. She is travelling through time while she holds me, this soft and moist life, so tiny, tiny in her arms. CRADLE is the word, cradle me in your arms, babe. But there is no lullaby, this is no romance.

Her friends visit us in the hospital, "this can't be a girl!" they chorus, and insist on checking. I have no choice, I can't even crawl away.

When I'm almost as tall as my father, he likes to say to relatives and friends at parties, "she's as tough as steel, we picked her up from the garbage." One of the times he gets mad at me, he grabs the steam iron, and swings out in a downward arc. The electric. The shock. The curved blade against my face. "Go to hell," I shout, and punch him in the face.

He's dead now, but the project isn't finished yet. Always at risk of being concussed into holy unconsciousness by falling debris, or of being pierced by rusty nails.

HARDHATS

AND

SAFETY BOOTS

MUST BE WORN

ON THIS PROJECT

Sometimes I forget, find myself naked as a newborn, stranded on a rocky beach, the sun shooting live wires of illumination down at me. Aaah, beautiful, the irony, they leave soon after you take your clothes off, ready for love. Cradle me in your arms, babe. I'm getting better at remembering, getting automatic about the hardhat and safety boots. But O, sometimes, some time, to feel rain gentle on my head, be sung a lullaby, as loving hands embrace my tired feet.

Bugis Street

I have faint recollections of how I had to walk close to my parents on that narrow street lit by kerosene lamps hung on hawkers' stalls. Customers slurped wonton noodles from large soup bowls, the ones laced with fish and rooster designs. At entrances of dark stairways leading up to rooms bathed in red light, men in gold lamé V-necklines plunging smooth chests, sucked cigarettes with crimson lips.

confluence of appetite
and secrecy
their perfumed mouths
and skin
in half-shadow
whispered a language
foreign, confusing.

I know Bugis
no longer exists
a lucrative romance
relocated in the name of progress.
walking East Hastings
in Vancouver now
I'm mistaken for a man,
passing people
on street corners
hustling for their lives and

I'm suddenly home again.
the hawkers' shouts receding
as I head into half-shadow.

Father:Mother:Tongue

For the longest time, when questioned about mother tongue, I replied "Hokkien," the Chinese dialect we spoke at home. "My father's father was born in Fukien province, and left for Southeast Asia in his thirties." How did the confusion arise, my father's power and presence overwhelming language, the truth of mother tongue? The mistake of connotation, to mean "what is familiar, original" by the word "mother"?

My mother's tongue is Hakka, a high-pitched eruption of sounds: *ni hee um hee, ngai mm hew ga gi hee*. Raised on the lower, sometimes sibilant, sometimes hazy register of my father's tongue, the meanings of hers were foreign, glimpsed almost as rarely as street accidents. Like those annual Chinese New Year visits with grandmother when I sat quietly observing the patterned tiles beneath my feet, listening through gaps for the occasional, recognizable word.

I never mastered father tongue, stumbling through tangled mazes in mind and mouth, the language trapped inside. *Wa bay hiaw kong, wa si-you chay chin kang kor.* I cannot remember a time I thought in Hokkien, it has always been English, the language of foreigners, of colonialism. Everything I think and write, does it truly belong to me then?

Mother's is not father's is not English is not mine.

Going to school a temporary escape from the confusion of mother's and father's tongues razing the air with the fire of resentment and malice. A fever which spread through my body, *delirium*. English, my adopted language, charging me out of one prison, into another.

Now, I apply myself to the task of a borrowed language, becoming mine, yet never mine. For whom is English an exclusive right, birthright, language entrenching a colony of values? To write, to make room with words, is to de-colonize, to lead the woman-child out of the labyrinth where she had been lost for lack of tongues.

Ni hee um hee, ngai mm hew ga gi hee — Are you going, I don't think I can find the way myself?
Wa bay hiaw kong, wa si-you chay chin kang kor — I don't know how to say it, I think this is very difficult.

TRANSLATIONS

Water

1. 水 *shui — water*

: a stream strokes and nudges
pebbles   snaking through
virgin landscape
until it meets
open river

: ripples, movement away
when stones strike

2. 淨 *ching — to cleanse...must go through an active*
   struggle with water

she bends towards
her feet in the water
hair matted with earth and
black bodies of insects

birds silent in the trees
leaves bristle in the wind: sound
ocean of her childhood
before she was sold

her hands stiff from the search
along this river
fingers feeling
cool crevices of rocks
lined with moss

her owner
brought her here when she was ten
she remembers
that twisted tree weeping branches
into water, the redness of this earth
rare and insistent, like the welt across
her face, swelling to a bulb
blood on her lips

now that he is dead
she returns
for her belongings

3. 沒 *mo — to dive, to sink in the water, to perish*

dazed from raw skin
licked by water
she opened her eyes to see him walk away
with the bundle: blood-stained clothes
box of seashells, the brass locket

he was taking away the last memory
her mother's gifts
her girl's voice useless
against pain, the blackness
of water

she reaches the waterfall, the place
he'd left his boots and rope
she undresses, warm
naked with present tense
dives into the deep green pool
under the thunder of water

4. 深 *shen — deep, profound*

world of slippery edges
uneven depths
this place enslaves
if only temporarily
it is not safe here, this false womb

reminds her of his power
even in death
power throbbing like a stubborn ache
in the narrow corridor between
conscious thought and skull-bone

I have survived, and still I must
plunge into the past

her hand finds softness
then hardness in a hole
pulls out a bundle of rags

5. 活 *huo — living...movable...moisture in the mouth is
   a sign of health and life*

that gasp of shock when air
rushes at the face
her lungs released
while her hand is clenched red
around the discovery: her own salvation

senses readjust
while rising from death
she moves up the rocks
slicing stillness with her wet body

a film of water lingers in the mouth
shoreline of her existence

The first Chinese symbol represents the element water, while each of
the subsequent symbols has 氵 (represents water), and other
characters. Word meanings are given by the combination of
characters.
Quotes from *Analysis of Chinese Characters* by G.D. Wilder and J.H.
Ingram, New York: Dover Publication, 1974.

Ⅰ Ⅰ   **47**

Translating Fortune: Cookie Wisdom

> Your love life resembles a
> tasty mess of noodles.

noodles
oodles of noodles

on birthdays
you cooked *mee sua* with
fresh liver and green onions
for good fortune
and longevity
i consumed dutifully
bloodied broth

to thread noodles
means
to gossip

    your chats with
    aunty from bukit timah
       how many wives did great-grandfather have?
          oh wasn't he a good provider?
       remember that young fellow
           on the third cousin's side?
         what did he do at his sister's wedding?
      never mind, she was
         poor
  what a shame!
      smooth complexion
        married to
  someone
    so black

tasty mmmm
fiction entangles
fact

watch animal eat
animal eat

> Of all forms of caution,
> caution in love is the most fatal.

romantic myths
fling caution to the winds

surrender to
those whom you want to
love you

the old hokkien movies
captivating
melodrama

noble heroine
surrenders
with tears and sighs and

at the washing well
commiserates with
other wives
half-confessing
abuse

in the town of lucheng
chen lin shi goes home
with clean clothes
to slaughter her husband
the butcher

mother, i never knew
i could love and still be free

did you?
do you?

if i bind my life for love
how far could i walk
before paralysis?

i was a kite
fading up to heaven
possessed by my lover's hands

how can an object fly
except by another's will?

i confess my ignorance

you didn't tell me
i could break shackles

fatal/love/caution

stop being prisoner
in my own house
that
i could walk away

> You can go wrong by being too skeptical
> as readily as by being too trusting.

helpless in your arms
i could go wrong
possession is nine-tenths
the law of love

meant to be seen not heard
meant to be smart in school
don't deviate from
the rationale of

i can't remember
if you ever held me
with your eyes

intelligence? what is that?
capture with
a line or net

with recognition

skepticism or

mummy

write with the tongue

i'm scared of
monsters in the closet

wish you could protect
against memory

i don't know which side of
shield me shield me   the wall

i am feeling

division between love and hate. wish you had shielded me.
too late to stop last night's dream, his penis
gesturing at me, you dazed by the kitchen sink.
his penis, twisted and upright, wrought iron spike.

> Love your enemies — it makes
> them darn mad.

tell me
how you define enemy

like the bible says
if i love when least expected
my enemy's head should rage
with hot coals

are those of us linked
by blood spared?
are only those who are
different
deserving of rage?
why call them into
one category?
why call us one?
i do and do not belong
with you

art of stretching past
the edge of
treason

oh i've tried

that jesus routine
knocking at empty houses

you said
mother love is hard
to change, you got more
than you deserve

i'm in love with
my enemy

she said
some of us are
far worse off than
 you women of colour
because we're working class
 what does it matter if
 we're white?

sunday i awakened
in muted sunlight and
burning tears

whose house is empty?
what does red mean?

translate also means: to remove to heaven
especially without death

translating fortune, act of disentangle.
from love and rage. leaping over walls, back into myself.

```
┌─────────────────────────────────┐
│   You will soon gain something   │
│     you have always wanted.      │
└─────────────────────────────────┘
```

                             (i am feeling

the many dreams of houses

outsider   the book says
looking for entrance   healing takes
afraid of what's inside   a whole life
peers through windows
keys don't fit

                                no straight lines
at the open door   or clear plot
wondering   it's a long haul
is there anyone   mother
who speaks my language?

                        who will walk with me?
                        who will dare taboo?

you are not there
         no one is

                   she said *i don't want to*

               (i am
                      translating

today
i dream i take possession
of my house and discover
in the hidden places
signs of
a concentration camp

dark planks of
bunk beds gleaming clean
faint smell
of bodies

where are the prisoners?
who's taken them away?

the dream/fortune   (i

All the fortune cookie sayings are actual found ones except the two
on page 54.
mee sua — extremely thin rice noodle
Incident in town of Lucheng based on fact, described in *The
Butcher's Wife* by Li Ang, Beacon Press, 1983.

Subject to Desire/Subject to Desire Too

Subject to Desire

1. mango

pressing against
supple orange flesh
juices escape
between fingers
mouth welcomes slippery softness
captured by tongue and teeth

the fragrance awakens memories
in ancient seats
of the brain

Subject to Desire Too

1. mango

she leans over the balcony, a typical tropical afternoon, her mangoes spilling out onto the street. sunlight melts her *cheong sam* until we, spectators below, desiring, grow our mouths large, long for juice from the sky to flood our tongues, sweet sticky monsoon. for everyone, a slightly different memory of feast, of flood. the fruit or the one who sucks, who is consumed?

cheong sam — close-fitting dress with slits up the sides

Subject to Desire

2. durian

in southeast asia
when it's durian season
crowds are grown on
that pungent, obstinate smell
fed on the anticipation
of rich yellow meat waiting
in chambers beneath
spiky barriers

hungry eyes and hands
for the ritual
knife splits open shells
buyers squat on sidewalks
gorge themselves under street-lamps

the durian is queen
invested with power
to intimidate and tantalize

Subject to Desire Too

2. durian

the three Chinese trishaw-drivers sit in the coffee shop corner of Koon Seng and Tembeling drinking sweet black *kopi*, imagine themselves with the women pinned up on the walls, Bunnies blonde blue-eyed barely clothed.

she drifts by in royal purple *sari*, with gold chains and bangles encircling her body, her eyes cast down on the pavement. they are curious yet uncomfortable with her softness. she drifts by, and they swear at her in Hokkien. she's Tamil, but she understands because her father brings these words home from digging ditches for the Public Works Department. the men call him a dark son of his mother's cunt. he comes home angry at his wife and children.

she drifts by, her *sari* a temporary armour, with places where cuts could be made toward her essence, her self.

kopi — Malay: coffee

Subject to Desire

3. tangelo

hybrid fruit
texture and colour of
an ordinary
orange
add a bump for defiance
miniature breast

I peel one
leisurely
spend an afternoon
arranging the single whorl
on black cardboard
composing for photographs

foetus or
unfurling frond

studies in
black-and-white
and Kodachrome

Subject to Desire Too

3. tangelo

finally alone she observes for her own pleasure. with the eyes, peel. loosen meanings, then compose. her own body, soft and taut at the same time, how it pleasures her! the beginning spirals out, endless. this private fantasy, while in the kitchen mother is cooking fish curry, her older sisters helping, her brother in his room listening to rock music. desire always new, her fruit its meaning transforms before her eyes and hands.

Subject to Desire

4. banana

penunguh is guardian
over the poor family's trees
punishes men and boys who steal
bananas or pee against the trees
by making the offending organ
swell to a painful blob

the key, of course, is to ask forgiveness

we eat bananas raw or deep fry them
place slices into coconut cream
desserts wrapped in leaves

long green plantains
with a bland taste
raw zucchini
others short and yellow
golden cores speckled
black, sweet as jam

whatever kind
they huddle on the stalk
seeking comfort
kept safe by *penunguh*
until their owners' hands
reach up

penunguh — Malay: guardian spirit of place and property

Subject to Desire Too

4. banana

she learns to desire the Other, fixate on male bodies, what they might look like or taste like. whereby they become a property of her mind, an object of her innocence, the place where confusion meets fantasy, how she could want the Other, while at the same time, shadows linger in the whispered stories of married women, the warning against trespass. desire and invasion, con*fused*.

Subject to Desire

5. mangosteen

a purple horsehair shell
size of a fist
spreading clasp of a thick green
calyx

inside
a globe
milky
kidney-shaped segments
hold their promise

you can't attack
as you might a watermelon

consequences
are serious
the juices leave indelible
stains

Subject to Desire Too

5. mangosteen

her cunt consumes. her lover's hand, fingers moving, being sucked squeezed milk of milky way boundaries no longer usual. definitions fail to hold, capture, the act of she consuming she. beware of she who captures, be reverent at her throne, she will not return the hand unstained.

Subject to Desire

6. cherry

see that cherry?
in the ad, poised
at the parting of red
lipsticked lips

you're supposed to lust
surmise she
wants me

you're supposed
to want this siren of a mouth
blood target

and the cherry
tight flesh
mean pit
is she
innocent
or
an accomplice?

Subject to Desire Too

6. cherry

she takes off her *cheong sam*, puts on sweatshirt and pants, black boots, rides the bus to the large billboard in the heart of Chinatown. Sunday 6 a.m. the day after Chinese New Year celebrations, streets deserted except for wooden crates spilling rotten persimmons, starfruits and the husks of durians. she pulls out the can of spray paint, and shoots the black jets of her anger toward the giant set of lipsticked lips, that foreign cherry, once-subject now background. art, its ability to obfuscate, or to transform, desire.

cheong sam — close-fitting dress with slits up the sides

A Taste for Blood

In the beginning was the word, and the word was with god, and the word was god.

This was the beginning, when truth came from another's mouth, salvation in the words of a text, frozen surface of a pond concealing secrets of the holy one. Then, another kind of surface. Inner curtain ripped by a cry from the womb, a wolf's lonely sound asserting: *in the beginning there was no fear, and then there was life.*

I write another life past this fear, to break the tyranny of other. *In the beginning, a sound against annihilation, the word.*

what is it about this night?
womb in which I curl
like a comma
waiting for conclusion

what daylight conceals
rises to power
under the moon

this longing for wolves
terror and
pleasure of being
hunted

blood rushes to my skin
at the sight of shadows

mostly mist in dream
why do I cry for you?

the curse of satan
in your childhood
your father's friends
who raped you and your brothers
then at eight
forced to pack a dead baby
in a sack of potatoes

these words a rusty crucifix
you plunged into me
> *you failed me twice*
> *my aggression is justified*
> *I am no longer a victim*

why do I cry for you?

I fear
while still drawn to
your instinct

           I don't give a fuck
           about your feelings

like the way
you don't see
the boundaries between
my flesh and yours

like the way they ate up
your childhood

take, eat this flesh
drink this blood

It was only when I became
a vampire that I respected
for the first time all of life....

I never knew what life was
until it ran out in a red gush
over my lips, my hands!

miracle conversion, how
a taste for blood transforms

this is familiar
I'm not sure why

small, powerless
I try to cooperate
as your prey
must sacrifice
take my body suck

desire is it
only about sex
or an ancient ritual?
my bones heavy sinking
into your dark purple sheets
my head floating above us
while you drain me
for the baby in the sack

Fritz Haarman killed boys
by biting on the neck
made sausages
he either ate or sold
in his butcher shop

James Riva shot his grandmother
drank blood
from the bullet holes

Jerry Moore consumed his girlfriend's
for strength, he said

the scent of perfume
sandalwood was mine
until you decided
to smell like me

              a warm summer's midnight
              you on the front porch
              smoke a cigarette
              inhale your mother's legacy
              while watching the Northern Lights

then you enter
make love to me in pitch black
drink me with urgency
our smells mix, concealed
skin to skin sex to sex
your kisses
roughened by smoke and memory

categories of good and evil

> at this moment
> I am unaware of them
> as your body turns in sleep
> toward me

how easy to surrender

> in twilight dream
> I want
> your unconscious smile
> to be reason for trust

> when does the wolf
> cease to suckle me?

how long before I uncurl
from you?

sometimes, like you
I dream of houses, being locked out
fearful even when
the door was open

a scent
web of hate for my own life
my body closing curls up
panic
at the entrance of love

I was also once
a cowering child

they chased me out
they called me witch

the place name changes
but the story recurs

you reclaim the name
revel in your anger and protest
I think of you as heroic
even holy
the unjustly treated martyr

a vessel
scars on clay
crude, glaring
from every direction

your staring blue eyes
your slender fingers
clutch the glass of scotch
your powerful cunt
shoots my belly
with warm fluid

two women remembering
did that make it more difficult
to separate?
my womb
hurting from the kicks
wish I could birth you
past torture

I know you better than you know yourself
you're abusive, you need to change
I have faith you'll improve

I failed to consider
you might be still
addressing your oppressors
I was in love
which meant
relinquishing

Kristen French, 15, was abducted on April 16, 1992, from a church parking lot in St. Catharines as she walked home from school. Her nude body was found two weeks later in a ditch in rural Burlington. An autopsy revealed that she had been assaulted sexually and asphyxiated. Police said she had been held captive for most of the time that she was missing.

Leslie Mahaffy, 14, was last seen at a convenience store near her home in Burlington on June 15, 1991. Parts of her body encased in concrete were found two weeks later in a lake near St. Catharines.

Globe and Mail, May 19, 1993

was it just a bad dream?
imagination?
does geography matter?
or is it more a question
of landscape?

                    the mirror reflects
                    no longer scary
                    the image of one
                    in daylight, clean
                    uncurled from my own
                    foetal helplessness

the Myth of Everywoman Everywhere
in a world of strangers
reading breathing terror
in the newspaper clippings you collect
details of violence
widespread and identical

but I don't want to be
another statistic

at first there were nightmares
I dismember you
the slashes repeated viciously
without hesitation
but you keep returning
like pieces of a jigsaw puzzle
drawn together
by some macabre spell

the image
my own eyes
no longer hollow orbits
penetrate the surface
my body finally solid again
molecules of light and dark
held together by necessity

years later
I hear about how
you repeatedly accuse others
of victimizing you

a survivor
runs out of the room
traumatized
by graphic details
of your story and you
proud to have such an impact

do we write only such truths?

seeing abusers in everyone else
except yourself
how heavy your pain
how hungry your eyes
veiled by
extreme intelligence

where is your mirror?

I return to the places we'd been
now no longer afraid
no longer
relinquishing

Return to the beginning. Begin to feel the particular. Gesture, not surface, not line. The comma becomes wolf stalking her own shadow. *Yea, though I walk through the valley of the shadow of death, I fear my own evil.*

There's a kind of hush all over the world tonight, all over the world you can hear the sound of. The kind of love known by silence, the omission.

And yet, possible to speak as if without words, my mouth uncurling text, god removed, the baby, the womb, surfacing to holiness. To pause in mid-language, to breathe.

"In the beginning was the word..." from the King James version of the Bible (John 1:1).
"Yea, though I walk through the valley of the shadow of death..." from King James version (Psalm 23:4).
"It was only when I became a vampire ..." from *Interview with the Vampire*, Anne Rice, Knopf, 1976.
"There's a kind of hush." Words and music by Les Reed and Geoff Stevens, 1966. Copyright Donna Music Ltd., London, England/Leo Feish, Inc. Sung by Herman's Hermits.

THE COLOURS OF HEROINES

Dreams of Lingerie
for Anna-Marie

looking for lost affection   in the aisle between
lust and true regard   haze daze down past brain talk
on the top shelf   what comes first   a dream or the experience of

silk?

the dream   post hypnotic suggestion of skin on

silk?

this is real   this real feel of cool on soft on

*

How did we begin this dialogue?   In one of our long-distance
desires to find answers, we discovered that common passion for
understatement.   Do some men talk this way about their Jockeys?
Do they thrill at the thought of black briefs?

*

there is always the perfect one   depending on mood   circumstance

the colours of heroines   want or fear

ovulate menstruate   quiver quake heat   jungle Jane releasing
eggs in her loins   that red hipster laughing
under the hide swinging fine vine   *oh baby baby*
so different from
the sensible cream cotton variety intent on
being invisible   pale nondescript   *please may I belong?*

did Joan of Arc own lingerie
being a virgin and off to war so often?

my grandmother, under her *baju panjang*
was hers different from his concubines'?

those myths: *The Faithful Harlot   The World of Suzie Wong*

my exotic Asian legacy demands

les liaisons dangereuses   I dream of the secret lace
black caressing my thighs   replacement?   anticipation?
or maybe a resonating hum *yes yes yes*
my body   in light and shadow plays

*

Do you think about your breasts sagging? The weight of the world.
They made such a deal about Atlas holding up the globe,
how would he have managed with two?

If you've got it, flaunt it. You remind me of the joy of underwire
bras, but I'm afraid of prominence. I remember how I slouched
through adolescence, depressed, acned, daunted by that
uncontrollable difference. Already I knew about male lust,
how I was responsible for leading them on, gee, I didn't want
that fame, so I tried to hold down those tiny tits with
cotton Maidenform.

Now, I'm starting to love the look of them. Sideways, front view,
and even plunge view. I dream of the day I reach them with my mouth,
tasting the joy of their texture. *Yahoo.* What fantasy.

*

it's about safe outrage   screaming moaning pleading
the politics of underwear   how to make a statement
one anonymous woman standing in a crowded subway car
tracking the Bloor line in Toronto
or flying from Calgary to Hawaii   the purple hearts on
her panties steaming

we women we desperate scared and sometimes killed or raped or
at very least treated like toys   pat pat on the head or bum
or crotch   see what happened to Linda Lovelace?

have we no privacy left?   a place of soft   of good feel

safe safe please

*

Did I ever tell you? On the day I "defended" my thesis
I took the morning ferry to Wolfe Island and back, watching the ice
break away from me on the currents. Then, I went to the S & R,
up to the third floor, women's section, and bought a pair of
French-cut bikini briefs. Black, with a white band of
Jockey Jockey Jockey all around. I wore them to the defence,
tasting victory.

Did I ever tell you? About the woman who showed me her breasts,
how drastically different they were, the right one much longer,
with the nipple swollen red from feeding her baby daughter.
Then, she hiked up her peach nightgown to show me
her Caesarean scar.

Truths, under the surface of things.

*

we were not there burning our bras in the sixties
we were newborns locked in diapers   you in Zambia
and me in Singapore   now we're here   towards
the end of a time   holding on gently to
our telephone receivers Calgary-Winnipeg-Calgary
sometimes the sound of animals
wail through pauses

what do women want?   you and me understand the landscape
of each other's desire   how different how similar
still
it is tenderness   the fact of a camisole   a dream
insisting itself   on your shoulder on mine

a dream walking that aisle
silk on silky skin

we talk through metaphors   the particulars of
conceal and reveal   delicate balance

line and breath and curve

baju panjang — form of dress mostly worn by Nonyas, women of mixed
Malay-Chinese descent.

"Women Running on the Beach"

for Christina Willings

painting tits in 1922
did Pablo really know about women
having a good time together?

ours is the kind of conversation
where outstretched arms
and bosoms spill
out of dresses daily.

last December
I brought you back
sand from English Bay,
and we cried
over Harvey's Bristol Cream.
trying on a conversation
about poetry and friendship,
our struggle against
concealment.

now that we live
in different cities,
I miss your coloratura
scaling the stairwell,
the hot Vietnamese Coffees
at Cafe Beano's
while pontificating
over glossy fashion magazines.
I miss the joy
of flexing biceps while jabbering

in postmodernist prose
in your kitchen.

I dream a language to survive
doubt or loss.
that freedom to run
amok on the beach,
not give a flying fuck
about the audience I dream
we outstrip even our own demons.
that we might write ourselves
rudely
off the canvas
naked, loose
uncensored.

Title based on painting of the same name by Pablo Picasso, 1922.

Red Sonja

are you ready for the she-devil with a sword?

in the original comic books Red Sonja is wild
red-maned warrior in chain mail bikini
unafraid of monsters or men
when she fought serpents conjured from her own fears
Gods of Vilayet! My own flesh attacking me
as if we were deadly foes!
she released herself from their grip
by letting her mind go blank

I'm introduced to her by Linda who's seen the movie
and fantasizes about the magic of this powerful woman
someone men respect and are slayed by in one way or another

I love Red Sonja's fashion sense, I could never be so bold

Linda who hooks for years on the streets
finally leaves her pimp and lover
sheds tight outfits for faded jeans and cotton sweaters
trains successfully as a welder
attends Al-Anon three nights a week
and finds peace at home with her cats

she shrinks her body into my large armchair
tells me in a hushed monotone the odds she's survived
as if it were no big deal
as if her own power didn't roar
like the she-devil's

Connie's Paradise Ltd.

Connie sits at her throne
white-and-black outfit chunky gold earrings

Connie's Paradise Ltd., Connie speaking, have you heard?
we have a faa-buulous extravaganza for newlyweds
get on the love wagon right now
wonderful deal, it's absolutely heavenly!

over-the-phone details about the Caribbean
down to the sexy lingerie waiting for
him and her on satin pillowcases

enter through pink organza enter paradise sunlight on weddings
framed photos of couples in tinted light
can you hear waves crashing on tropical sand?

Connie is the heroine your mother dreams about
a saviour for worrisome sons or daughters
I hear her through the walls
seductive moan of saxophone sound
while the woman in my office cries
her husband sits in front of the T.V.
with a bag of nachos and a six-pack

I conjure up stories about Connie:
she left her husband after fifteen years
tired of ironing his dress shirts
ran off with the fitness instructor
a wild fling, a great suntan

convinced afterwards she could market paradise
or at least two weeks of it

so how about it, Connie, for me and my girlfriend?
what kind of welcoming party at the hotel?
what kind of lingerie?
will there be genuine acceptance for Eve and Eve?
orchids strewn on the path up to the lavender bed
plums and mangoes in crystal bowls on lace tablecloth
warm sand   breasts lolling   warm sand
splendour without fear or violence

weather permitting, Paradise?

Belly Ache

Nina travelled
from Hamilton to Crete
kept herself sane by belly-dancing
imagine her Rubenesque body
coiling and heaving
her flesh rippling desire
in her audience

at a party, after eight beers
she disclosed she used to cut herself
small knife wounds
on her belly, then deeper and deeper
until fear stopped her
she never said if she quit dancing
or if she covered her abdominal area

once, while changing in the Y locker room
I glimpsed the faint keloids
like children dancing 'round
her navel, crescent
moons wanting sun
as we slipped back
into street-clothes
I pondered her secret universe
I could only say
you like taking risks
don't you?

Lady Precious Stream

you who defied big daddy the Prime Minister
who chose love instead of class
married the poet-gardener who left
for war in the Western Regions
and showed up eighteen years later

Lady Precious Stream
did you exist in more than the play?
the years of scarcity in your humble cave
speaking only words of tolerance
waiting for your lover to avenge your suffering
resisting a mother's plea to return to luxury

Lady you also lived in my childhood
the woman who collected our compost in tinbuckets
as Ah Mui you ironed my clothes and baby-sat
as my mother you hunched over the washboard
furiously scrubbing socks and underwear
you appeared three years ago in my dream
the gift: a pearl melting to liquid warmth down my back

if you returned today
and checked out the state of affairs for women
would you be R.E.A.L. or F.A.K.E.?
would you count all women as sisters?
would you starve yourself to fit tight leggings?
would you read trashy novels or watch soaps?
would you masturbate?
would you take an auto mechanics course or
buy a dirt bike cruise the streets at dusk?

would you spend two decades wondering?

Based on play of the same name by H.L. Hsiung, 1962.

Orchid Riddles

the heart of an orchid
is a cave

exuding a sweet scent of nectar

the heart of a cave
is an orchid

warm memory after
love on the stone floor

to find the cave you must
understand the orchid's heart
she thrives on humidity
appears on virtually every continent
dressed in a different costume
each time

to woo the orchid you must
locate the secret
entrance
touch her brooding
colourful lip
gently just so
a measured pressure

she will silence you with
her coming
release
magic in your fingers

Angels Smiling

so tell me, is this as real
to you as it is to me?
this waking up early, or
not sleeping at all
aching with desire
while angels guide us
through songs or a joke.
remember that free desk you needed
waiting for us in the alley?
in one of the drawers we found
a photograph of an Asian woman,
as well as a fortune cookie:
you think that is a secret
but it never has been one

now, this distance.
trembling for hours after
your voice over the phone.
this absence measures my slow
thought unwinding its serpentine
length, sleek instinct
crossing borders to tongue you.

I want to exclaim to you in person
when alone threading *kairos*
with our fingers
that angels are real
visiting
to gift us with magic
a certain look or sigh
opening the moment to eternity.

what can I say now
when the air in my lungs is both
light and heavy with missing you?

my angel smiling

kairos — Greek: denotes timing or timelessness or the fullness of the present, as contrasted with *chronos* which refers to the chronological sense of time.

How Many Families?

special of the week
so there's a quota:
only one allowed per family.
at the supermarket checkout
you hear the Asian man
with the two chickens insisting,
two addresses
points to the woman beside him.
the cashier doesn't seem
to hear or understand.
his brown fingers
punch in
the price for one, disregard
the two I.D.s and the repeated plea.

you're angry and come to the rescue
don't you understand?
they live in two homes
they even have proof.
you arrive home feeling ashamed
you hadn't gone to the management,
stunned that racism
has worn you down so deeply.
memories of
your parents being ignored
because of their skin and accent
their Chinese-ness.

your own earlier self-hatred
reflected in the cashier's
eyes cast downward at
his flying fingers.

System of Stars

Sound of the ocean, the ssssound asleep and then rising up like a serpent, while we watch for shooting stars. Somehow it seems like a different universe, because it's Point-No-Point on the Island, here the Milky Way is easily visible, here the stars can be recognized.

We weave through trails, our small flashlights two circles of light. You notice my furtive glancing to left and right, the questions about bears. *I was afraid of the dark as a child*, I tell you. Creatures I didn't understand, their appearance from out of the shadows sudden, unannounced. Arms around each other, you encourage me to trust, to look up for shooting stars while you transport me along the path. It is dizzying, the galaxy shifting as I move, losing sense of ground, the sound of ocean hypnotic, certain, as I feel reality shift upwards.

On a red bench, my head nestles in your lap. Behind us, spurts of light, perhaps the lighthouse on Bluff Point? I watch the northern sky for a long time before I see my first shooting star. You seem surprised I had never seen one before tonight. You ask, *do you think there are other forms of intelligent life out there, do they try to make contact with us?* As in, the generic us? Or, us two women, out here waiting, with our questions? I remember the T.V. episodes about U.F.O.s, but somehow they said nothing about this moment, the lightness I feel inside. This universe: a kind of knowing, an openness to trust, before the child learned fear, where darkness holds only promise of discovery, adventure. Your body, the cosmos, me.

On Lok

A greasy spoon, with Chinese waitresses in red uniforms pouring jasmine tea from Melitta flasks, serving a mix of rowdy customers. We've met here many times before, to read the same section of the menu, to select rice noodles almost every time. With soya sauce chicken and wontons.

On Lok. In Cantonese, 安 樂 means peace and happiness. Try to exist together, pairing without loss, is it possible? We met in speed of light, light-years ago, maybe we were two Chinese women then too.

In my homeland, "coffee shops" housed men who hitched legs up on chairs, drank strong black coffee sweetened with condensed milk, and spat occasionally into spittoons under the marble-top tables. Women had no place to be outrageous together. Except when cooking or eating. This is still how our lives prosper by the moment, unfolding with each detail of how it tastes, what possibilities come to mind because of memory. You tell me how your mother made wontons with wide wings, so that eating them was truly "swallowing cloud." As I listen to your story, I am slurping, slurping, the slippery delightful around my tongue down my throat.

Where are my wings now in this new city with you?

Speed of talk, English words racing between us. We check if the other had a similar phrase in her dialect.

Even though some might think us sisters or that we look alike, we often wait for the bridge, sometimes strain to build one. You offer the phrase: *I only have to look at you with one eye, and it's as if you were a glass bottle.* Am I so transparent? I know we tried to be together in another life, limited then by being concubines to one man. Perhaps this is what brings tears to your eyes and words: *You had a very difficult life.*

I believe in destiny, that home arrives again and again, and our hidden senses recognize.

Speed of light, travelling to this present and On Lok, where the waitresses are red dots moving through the confusion around us.

wonton — Chinese: to swallow cloud

Peranakan

I didn't know *peranakan* was also mine.

There'd been no claiming, no recognition of that identity in my home. My mother's mother born in Riau, Indonesia, a *Nonya,* meant she wasn't just Chinese. Her *baju panjang*, transparent lace-top drawn shut with gold pins, heavy ornate gold belt held up her sarong. But she didn't chew betel nut, like her mother. My father's relatives insisted they were truly pure, but why then the dark skin, the thick, sensual lips?

Late one night, everything changed. With or without consent, a Chinese merchant forays into a *kampong*? Or was it the Malay man who dared to fall in love with a Chinese woman? Malays, the indigenous people, hunted and fished, before the myriad settlers from China drifted southward to seek their fortune. The Chinese despised the Malays, called them *huang na*. Savages. In fact my parents spoke of them as if they were inferior, as if we shared nothing in common.

Would they have recognised and spared us during the race riots? Me and my father coasting along on the scooter, dodged their wielded *parangs* a hundred feet away. *A miracle*, he would say for years after, how a truck swerved and blocked the way, giving us just enough time to escape.

Peranakan/Nonya/Baba: seldom used in my home. Verbal exchanges in the market early in the morning,

Hokkien and Malay and English all strung together as mother haggled over the price of *ikan* and vegetables.

Travelling in China with my white girlfriend, two men in Guangzhou on the bus spoke in Cantonese, thought I didn't understand. *Look at her clothes. Look at the front of her head, those blonde streaks, one of her parents must be Japanese, the other white.* Some places, they knew me as Chinese and asked me to relay requests. I was obviously the white person's interpreter.

In Vancouver she said *you have a peranakan face, just like mine.* The first time I am ever recognised as a mixed breed. Evidence of crossed borders. If I speak Hokkien, if I speak Malay, if I label myself one race or another, does that fix my identity? To spend years confined to one niche, and then *peranakan* manifests on the tongue and skin. What makes the night, the absence of day? What moves truth ahead, changing and yet eternal?

peranakan — Malay: local born but also refers to *Babas* and *Nonyas,* respectively, males and females of Malay-Chinese descent.
baju panjang — form of dress mostly worn by *Nonyas,* women of mixed Malay-Chinese descent.
kampong — Malay: village
huang na — Hokkien: savage
ikan — Malay: fish

ACKNOWLEDGEMENTS

Some of these poems have appeared in the following publications:

absinthe

Contemporary Verse 2

Descant

Grain

Many-Mouthed Birds: Contemporary Writing by Chinese Canadians

More Garden Varieties Two: An Anthology of Poetry

The New Quarterly

West Coast Line

Zine But Not Herd

TRANSLATING FORTUNE: COOKIE WISDOM was performed, with the participation of Nancy Cullen, at Exquisite C.O.R.P.S.E. in Calgary, February 1992.

WATER was performed at Tapestry, Vancouver, March 1992.

I am grateful to many friends. Thanks to the Monday night writers' group in Kingston for the great literary criticism and support. Daphne Marlatt, Roberta Rees: thank you for inspiration. Thank you, Carmen Rodriguez and Nancy Richler, for many helpful comments on some of the poems. Angela Hryniuk: for your encouragement, editing expertise and respect!

And Suemay Black, thanks for the sustaining humour and companionship.

Nora Patrich is a painter who submerges her palette in her theme, someone for whom creation is a ritual incarnated in her. An Argentinian who lives in Canada, Nora Patrich's work is marked by Latin American roots, and maintains the dream of preserving those roots through a realism that seeks deep into the pysche of a woman. Her work has been widely exhibited in Canada and internationally, and several of her pieces have been purchased by major museums in Argentina. Nora Patrich lives in Vancouver, B.C.

Photo: Suemay Black

Lydia Kwa was born in Singapore and came to
Canada in 1980. She has lived in Toronto, Kingston
and Calgary. She now makes her home in Vancouver,
working as a writer and a therapist. Her work has
appeared in various literary journals and anthologies
including *Many-Mouthed Birds: Contemporary
Writing by Chinese Canadians. The Colours of
Heroines* is her first book.